LEAD WITH MOJO

7 STEPS TO BECOMING THE LEADER OTHERS WANT TO FOLLOW

Plus 3 Career-Boosting Bonus Steps!

MANAGER MOJO

STEVE CALDWELL, THE MOJO MENTOR

www.ManagerMojo.com

ISBN: 978-1539933342

First Printing: December, 2016

Published by 102nd Place LLC
Scottsdale, AZ 85266

Table of Contents

FOREWORD

I am a woman who has been in the business world for forty awesome years. I have loved it!

Like many of you reading this book, I entered my first career wanting to do my best and prove myself. I didn't think it would lead to a promotion so quickly, far before I felt ready. I assumed people were seeing something in me that I couldn't see for myself.

And then there was another promotion (far before I was ready) and another. I didn't feel ready for those either.

I really didn't know how to lead my team. Each day I was just eking it out, doing the best that I could.

When I met Steve Caldwell eight short years ago, all of a sudden I was seeing what leadership truly meant. I wish I had his knowledge and insight when I was in the depths of my career climbing the ladder. I could have been a much better leader and I could have developed future awesome leaders.

Yes, I am prejudiced and biased because Steve is my husband. But you don't have to take my word for it. All I ask is that if you have been struggling in your management career, wishing you were one of those leaders who made it look easy, read this book! **Lead with Mojo** will provide you clear, simple, actionable information that you can begin to implement immediately.

Your career is an important part of your life. Make it all that you want it to be, earn the lucrative salary awarded to great leaders, and create the life that you desire.

Here's to Your Leadership Mojo!

Cindy Caldwell

INTRODUCTION

Let me be honest with you. When I began my career and received my first promotion, I was clueless about what a good manager should do. I did all the wrong things, and I truly was a bad manager. Not just because I didn't know, but no one told me! My boss didn't tell me (he probably didn't know either), and there was no such thing as far as I knew as a 'coach' or a 'mentor.'

This book, *Lead with Mojo – 7 Steps to Becoming the Leader Others Want to Follow,* is to share with you the insights I've had over the years of why I was so bad, and most importantly, to share with you the lessons learned that have allowed me to become a great manager and leader.

I'm the prime example – "Leaders are made, not born!"

Having grown up in management, I understand how crunched you are for time. So each chapter of this book has been designed to be read in 15-20 minutes, a minimal investment of time yet enough to have a great insight which can impact your career. Read all seven chapters, and you are well on your way to becoming "The Leader that Others Want to Follow!"

Plus, because you have made an investment in your career by purchasing this book, I'm going to make a further investment in *you*. At the end you will find *3 Bonus Steps* that, if implemented, will allow you to flourish as an awesome manager and leader!

Read these tips, and you will be on the way to becoming the manager your employees respect and love working with. Here's to developing great Mojo!

Steve Caldwell

CHAPTER ONE

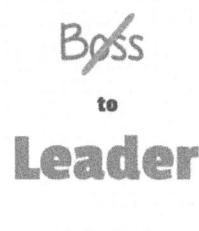

YOU THINK BEING THE BOSS MEANS SOMETHING

When you first become a manager, when you're now the boss, you feel that great things are in store for you. All of a sudden you feel like you're really important. People are starting to act like they are listening and you become the 'man' or the 'woman' that everyone is coming to for advice. They are coming to you for permission. They are coming to you for your recommendations. It can be a little heady when you first become a manager, because all of a sudden you have all of this so-called power. Your ego gets inflated.

It can and often does become overwhelming. It can be an enticing aphrodisiac to get this title of 'The Boss,' and it is the most deceptive type of energy that I know of.

This energy can be either positive or negative, and when it goes over the top it becomes negative. What happens is that the manager begins to believe that everyone is hanging on to every word they have to say.

When you think about it, all you have to do is tap into the sports world to look for examples of how this happens. People all of a sudden become stars in sports, and everybody starts writing about them. They tell them how great they are and how wonderful they are. The problem for the sports figures is that they start believing this stuff. They begin to think that everybody wants them; everybody thinks they're wonderful and they can do no wrong.

They begin to actually believe all the accolades. We call it 'letting it go to their heads.' When that happens they begin to *lose* their head. They aren't as effective as they once were.

The very same thing happens to us in management. We get all of this positive attention at the beginning. We get hooked on it and we think it's always going to be like this. The fact is, it's not, and we have to earn that 'Boss' title.

But most of us aren't trained on how to recognize when we're becoming bossy and when the 'boss syndrome' sets in. So what I want to do is give you a couple of thoughts about how you can help determine if the boss syndrome is hurting you.

I want to give you a few questions to examine and correct for yourself.

The first one is, how much additional work are you doing right now? In other words, are you doing not only your work but are you doing some of the work for your team that really should be somebody else's? Are you doing tasks that could easily have been assigned to or done by someone else? If you find yourself doing some of these things, then it's likely you're already on the edge of the boss syndrome.

Another good question to think about is if you find yourself giving permission to your people every day. Does every little decision have to come to you for your opinion? If that is happening, then you've begun to acquire the boss syndrome, instead of being a great leader and a great manager.

Do you find yourself having to tell people what to do and when to do it? A lot of managers walk around and say "My people aren't doing anything. They're just sitting around doing nothing. If I didn't come around and tell them what to do, they wouldn't do a thing." If you are making those kinds of statements or you know someone who is, you know they have gotten deep into the boss syndrome. Bigger problems are in the future for that individual.

Another good way to look at whether or not you're becoming too bossy is whether you are beginning to work long hours, at a point where you can't seem to get anything done and you're beginning to take work home with you because you can't get it done at work. Are you beginning to do stuff on the weekends? Do you feel like you're never having any time for yourself to think, plan and encourage other people? If you are, you can bet you're already in the middle of being 'the boss' and having the boss syndrome.

It's going to cause you more and more problems if you're answering these questions 'yes,' because what's going to happen is you're going to reach a period of resistance and burnout that is going to hurt you. You're the boss, but you don't have to be the boss of *everything*.

You have to learn how to delegate what I call 'real authority.' What do I mean when I say 'real authority'? Most people believe that when they assign a task to somebody they've assigned them the authority to get that task done. Too many managers, i.e.: Bosses, give an employee a task, but they want you to do it exactly like they would do it. When you're doing that, you're not really giving that person the authority to complete the task the way that they think. They're doing it the way that you want it done.

That rarely works. What you need to begin doing is explain the scope of the authority that you're giving them. Tell them where they can make decisions and encourage them to make the decisions on their own moving forward without having to come back to you.

Most beginning managers struggle with this, because they worry about giving them too much authority and they are making a mistake. If you're going to be a great leader, you have to be able to accept mistakes sometimes. You have to be able to let them get things done in a way that feels good to them. You can't always say that everything needs to be done exactly the way you want it done. If you do, you will find you'll lose that person's creativity. You're going to lose their heart. You're going to lose their brain. You're not going to be leading; you're going to be dictating.

All that does is slow down the process. Give them the authority, explain the scope of the authority, then let them go and do it.

Real authority is, in my opinion, the most difficult thing for managers to delegate. A mature manager is willing to accept a few mistakes along the way. Real authority is the most difficult to delegate at all levels of an organization, from CEO down to front line managers.

Managers are so unwilling to delegate authority. Instead, what they do is delegate tasks, and then they slow everything down by requiring employees to ask permission along the way. What they get is an end result that was painstakingly slow to arrive at. They get a result that doesn't look very creative or quality oriented.

This actually means that all you've got in your own organization is whatever creativity that leader happens to have. Employees' unique talents are missed. CEO's often wind up crippling their organization because they can't see that they have talented people all around them.

The job we have as managers and leaders is to build people up. If you can't build them, you can't help to them perform at the highest levels. Learn to delegate real authority, stop being 'the boss' and start being their teacher, coach, and mentor.

This is a very personal thing for me, because I felt overwhelmed before I really understood what I was doing. I was doing things that should have been done by others. I wasn't being as productive as I should have been. I was telling people what to do and how to do it, and productivity began to crash. Once that happened I realized that I couldn't keep doing what I was doing. I had to begin to let go, and I had to rethink my approach.

I began to realize the key to successful management is in trusting other people and letting them do their job. I began to leverage their strengths, strengths that I didn't have, and I began to realize that I was getting so much more done. I began to understand the concept of using other people's strengths to get things done. Before that, I'd never understood that other people had strengths that were far superior to my own. A great leader understands that. You have to be able to understand that other people have talents as well.

No one person is the perfect boss. You've got to be able to leverage other people.

I began to understand and I began to get my life back. I got my joy back, and I began to get things done in a way that got results. Once I understood this, employees still wanted to call me 'the boss,' but now I would tell them, "You know, I appreciate that thought, but I'm in the trenches here just like you are and I depend on you to help us get stuff done."

My job was to coordinate, not to do everything, but to help them and let them help me. The more I trusted and delegated, we all learned. Actually, more people wanted to call me 'boss.' But the difference was, the tone was different. There was more affection. They were more trusting. They were more giving.

The lesson is to understand that you can get all the respect, the ego and all of those things that make you feel good about being the boss, but it's so much better when people feel like they are able to be their own boss as well. It is a mature person who begins to understand this. When you do, great things start to happen.

So I want to tell you, please don't let the boss syndrome kill your success. I see it so often, and it's disheartening that people with real talent and real ambition get derailed because they can't figure out how to delegate real authority with the task. They have decided that they'll use the power of their position to be 'the boss' and they force everyone into complying.

I've got to warn you, the higher you rise in management, the more essential that it is.

You have to be able to trust others. You have to be able to grow others. You have to be able to stretch others. You have to quit being the boss that requires they come to you for everything. Be the boss that gives them the power to make their own decisions.

Start practicing this fine art of trusting others and delegating real authority today. If you do, you're going to have great things begin to happen in your career and in your life. You're going to be a great manager with a great career ahead of you.

CHAPTER TWO

The relationship between boss & team is critical to their success

YOU ONLY CRITICIZE NEVER COMPLIMENT

This section could also be titled, "I gave you a compliment six months ago, what more do you want?"

I know, I know. Some of you are laughing already and some are probably saying, "Yeah man! That's right. What's the big deal?"

But if you really want to be a great leader, you have to master some simple forms of communicating with people.

Let me begin by sharing a story with you. I used to work with a man who had incredible talent and incredible gifts. He was a great salesman, and he was always at the top of the list. Like most superstars, he was recognized and eventually offered a promotion. He took the job managing people, and he believed that he would quickly master the art of management. After all, he'd been a great salesperson and he thought he knew everything about sales, he thought he knew everything about people, and management would just be one more step in the rungs of his career ladder to great success.

When he was in sales, he understood the meaning of establishing a relationship. After all, he was darn good at it as the results showed. He found creating relationships with prospects quite easy to do. However, what he didn't realize was that the relationships created in sales were vastly different than those he would need when people reported directly to him.

He needed to understand that real relationships, ones not just based on sales interactions, but real relationships with people who were reporting to him would require much more effort on his part.

But he didn't like all of what he thought were touchy-feely kinds of interaction. He just wanted results. So he preferred to tell people what to do. He'd tell them when to do it. He'd tell them *how* to do it. You get the idea I'm sure. You may have worked for one of these people and, hopefully, you're not one of them.

You see, he was one of those types of people who was quick to criticize and slow to compliment. He was constantly on the lookout for something that he perceived somebody was doing wrong. He thought that his job as manager was to correct that ASAP. He would look for those opportunities; he would correct people and get them back onto the right path as defined by him.

This worked for a while, but his problem was that even when his people changed their behavior he rarely recognized their effort or accomplishment. He just took it for granted. So he wouldn't compliment them.

Over a period of time he started to go over the line. Here's how he did it. When somebody on his team would have a great win, he started to make comments in front of other people like – "Yeah, that's great.

But if you'd have listened to me earlier, you would have had even more success, and you would have had it quicker."

Think how you would react if that were you and your boss was saying that to other people in front of you. The thing was, he didn't do it just to one person. He did it to everybody.

It wasn't long before his team, hearing this type of left-handed compliment, was completely disengaged. Not only were they not motivated, they began to openly cause dissention. His lack of real concern for others had laid a foundation of mistrust, unhappiness and lack of productivity. Management was left with no other choice than to fire him.

The sad thing is, even after being fired, he had no real clue as to what had happened. He would tell people things like, "I don't really like management anyway. All people do is whine and complain about what they don't have. I'd rather just be responsible for me and avoid all these complainers in the future."

Wow! You see, what he didn't understand was that this situation was totally avoidable and he could have done it with some simple communications principles, but he just didn't get it. He just didn't care.

This is an example that I've witnessed, but I have to tell you it is going on in the workplace all over the world. Disengagement in the workplace has never been higher as evidenced by a survey Gallup continues to do year after year. Do you know that only 20% of the people that work for you are actually engaged? They are those who want to be able to be at work. They are happy to show up. They are happy to do their jobs.

But literally, 80% of the people who are there either are showing up only because they need a check, or they've already decided to leave and just haven't found another job yet.

It doesn't have to be this way. Let's change this. Let's create engaged workers, and let's be great leaders.

I believe that if you're going to be a great leader, one of the most important skills you have to master and be committed to is communication. Let's talk about how you can be a great communicator.

I've found that people get confused when I teach communication. People think I mean that you must be extremely precise in all your verbal and written communications with your team. Now, that's good. It's good to be extremely precise in all your communications, verbal or written. But that's not what I'm talking about.

The low detail people, on the other hand, rather than focusing on that precision, they believe I'm talking about how nicely you tell people what you need to have done. For them, it's about being overly friendly or over the top. You've just got to be nice to people. But you know what, that's not what I'm talking about either.

You see, when I refer to communication, I want you to think of it differently. I'm going to give you one simple word that I want you to think about whenever we're talking about communication.

That simple word is *connection*. Connection is the skill of demonstrating and expressing genuine concern for the other person. You see, connection is what most managers are missing with their team.

Managers can tell me what they are good at, and they can tell me what their people are good at. And they can tell me what their people aren't good at. But when I ask a manager to tell me what the real dreams, desires, and hopes of the members of their team are, they look at me with a blank face. They simply say "How the heck am I supposed to know that? No, I don't know what their real dreams, real desires, real hopes are. After all, we're here to do a job. My job is to manage, their job is to get stuff done, and no, I don't know that. Is that even necessary?"

In short, what they are telling me is that there is no real connection to their team members. They just don't know who they are working with. If you don't know those things, you don't really know the people that you're working with. You might know a little bit about their habits. You may know a little bit about their attitude, but frankly you just don't know *them*.

We all get like this today. Let me ask you, do you even know the names of all your neighbors? I'll bet you don't. I'll bet none of us does. The fact is, it is so rare today in our world to really *know* people.

We live in a society that believes that simply showing a polite gesture is good enough. We refuse to get involved with people. We don't want to know what their problems are. We don't want to know what their dreams are. We don't want to know what their real desires are. For most of us, we don't even know what our *own* are. So, we wind up disconnecting.

You see, we live in this polite world, but that's not the real world. Great leaders are <u>*always*</u> involved. They always understand the true motivation of every single member of their team. They've had conversations about it. They've had discussions. They've worked on plans to try and make sure their people understand how to move ahead.

You see, those great leaders express genuine concern for their people, and even more importantly, they actually express genuine joy on every success that their team member has. They get this simple principle – it's all about *them* and it's not about you.

You have to take joy in what other people do; otherwise, you're missing out on one of the greatest blessings of being in management. If you're going to truly love being a leader and love being a manager, the fact is you have to know your people. You have to know what is important to them. You've got to genuinely be concerned so that they can experience it.

There is nothing in a great leader's mind that is better than seeing someone they have helped achieve one of their main goals. How cool is that?! It's awesome, and a great feeling. It gives you so much energy, and it gives you the energy that you need to go into those infinite meetings that you have to attend. Because you know when you go back you're going to have a real connection with the team members, and you're working together to achieve your goals. It is an awesome feeling!

The problem is, most managers never experience that feeling because they don't have real connections at work. They have direct reports. They have human beings with names and numbers associated to them, but other than that they are not connecting with them.

I want to challenge you today to examine your own actions. Are you expressing thanks to your team members every time they do a great job? If not, then why not? Do you think that you're too busy? Do you think they don't really need that compliment?

If you do think that, I want you to consider that study after study has shown that parents who do not compliment their children on accomplishments create children that search for real love and attention all their lives and rarely find it. These people are rarely happy in their life.

We've done the same thing in business. We ignore the simple fact that we must connect with and compliment people when they do a great job. Therefore, by not doing these things, we are creating an environment where our people are constantly searching for somebody who cares about what they do. The reality is we spend so much time at work, isn't it logical that we would need somebody to really care about what we do? And isn't it logical that they should express gratitude for what we've done? And isn't it logical that somebody would actually care about those things that we spent extra time and effort and energy on to get right?

I would say absolutely! We all want that. We all need it. People need compliments.

They need connection. They need to know that the small stuff counts. Great leaders never miss an opportunity to point out something good. Your rule should be to compliment 10 times as much as you criticize. Write that down and remember it. *Your rule should be to compliment 10 times as often as you criticize.*

Yes, I'm aware that it opens you up personally to disappointments on occasion, but that's the price you have to pay for great leadership. You've got to be willing to compliment all of the small accomplishments. You can't wait for the big accomplishments, and decide to compliment now since it's been three months since the last one. That is not a connection, and the person who is working with you is going to think you don't care or that you felt obligated to say something because it was a big deal.

You have to be open in order to be the great leader that you need to be. You have to be open in order for your team members to be open. You either have to connect, or by default, you're going to create disconnect. The choice is up to you. You get to make that choice because you're the leader; you're the person in the management seat. You're the person who is responsible.

Connection is the bridge that creates that desire in people to reach out to get clarification from their boss. Connection is what creates the extra motivation to stay late, to give a little extra attention to a key project. Connection is what causes people to show initiative whenever it's necessary.

You see, they care about what you think as their leader, and therefore, they will consider that and they will give you that little bit of extra that you're not paying for. It's inside of them. It's there. It's up to you to motivate them to get it out. Real connection starts small and it grows.

Let me give you a couple of examples. It could be something as simple as 'Hey, I noticed you came in early all five days this week. I really appreciate it!' That's a simple, quick statement. It doesn't have to be anything more than that.

How about, 'Thanks for always taking that extra time to proofread your report. It's so nice to be able to depend on you to get your reports right. I always enjoy looking at them.' You could say, 'I love your idea on solving that problem we had. You have great ideas and you always go the extra mile. Thank you for doing that.'

Remember this simple thing. There's nothing small when real connection exists, especially when it's expressed along with a genuine concern for that person. But you've got to know that person. You've got to connect with them. You've got to know their dreams, their desires, their goals, and that comes from actually having conversations and asking them their opinion.

When you create these connections, this is how your team is going to come to like you, respect you, and yes, even to love you. I know for some of you, you think 'My team might love me?' Of course they would, because they would be able to say that yes, I know I spend a lot of time at work, but I'll tell you what, I've got an awesome boss. I've got a great situation. He/she cares about everything that I do. He/she always tells me. He/she tells me all the time when I'm doing a great job, and I'm telling you, I'm not going to let him/her down. I'm going to be there.

That's when you know that you've been able to achieve your goal to be the leader others not only want to follow, but they want to emulate. We need more managers like that. We need more leaders like that.

I know you can do it. I challenge you to do that today. Begin noticing the small successes of your employees, and offer them a sincere compliment.

CHAPTER THREE

YOU DON'T GIVE CLEAR DIRECTIONS

Giving clear directions is another important skill to develop as a manager. You have to be able to communicate effectively to your team in order for your team to succeed. Unfortunately, most of us think we are superstars at this, and the reality may be far from what our personal opinion is.

Here's what I'd like for you to think about. When you give clear directions, here are the top 3 benefits:

1) It saves time for you

You are a busy person. Being in management is a tremendous demand on your time each day, every day. It seems like there's never enough time to give your full attention to all of the things that need to be done. When you incorporate today's meeting culture where everybody wants to meet half the day as well as expect you to get all your work done it becomes incredibly difficult, and you need to find ways to save time.

One of the biggest benefits of giving clear directions is that it saves your personal time and allows you to be more effective in the areas that you need to be effective.

2) It saves time for your employees

So many employees really want to get the job done. They want to do their job effectively, but we in management don't give clear directions and therefore we're wasting their time as well. You want to improve both your productivity and the productivity of your team.

3) It helps achieve your goals faster

This is the benefit that I like the most, because goals are being achieved faster when you're giving clear directions. People have marching orders. They know exactly what needs to be done. It is up to you to determine what the team needs to do and in what order. People like to know priorities. They want you to help them understand exactly what is the most important to move the business forward at that particular time. It helps all of us.

Maybe you're like me and you struggle with this. I have to tell you, I had so much difficulty with this and I still struggle with it, even after all the years being in management. I still struggle with giving directions clearly. Possibly my problems are similar to some of the things you've experienced. Here are some examples:

I talk too much.

I ramble around. I'm not specific. I don't give enough of the specific, pertinent details that allow people to clearly understand what I'm thinking. I'm not naturally a high-detail person, so I have to constantly remind myself to slow down, think about what I need to do. What are the key steps?

I tend to shoot from the hip – or what I would call 'freelance.' Something needs to be done, I'll say we need to get this done but I don't really explain what needs to be done, or the reason it needs to be done, or what I see as the possible steps. What I do is basically say 'get this bottom line,' but I don't fill in enough of the information around it, so people have to try and guess what I'm thinking.

I hope you understand that anytime you're getting someone to guess what you're thinking you've got a problem. I tended to do that quite often early in my career and I still do it occasionally.

I move too fast.

The other thing that I do is move too fast. Many managers move too fast. We have so many things on our agenda each day that we move so fast we don't give the time that's needed to express clearly what needs to be done.

The fact is, what we're doing is not estab-lishing priorities. So we substitute moving fast and not giving the time as an excuse for not getting things done. Because frankly no one really knows what the most important thing to do today is.

So we are moving way too fast.

People absorb data differently.

I assumed early in my career that people understood what I was saying. I thought that if I gave them just enough information they'd figure it out for themselves. Because that's what I'd do with other people, I thought everyone else did as well.

I didn't really listen clearly to other people. I'd listen to what I thought I understood, and then I would make my own decisions and do it the way I wanted to. That doesn't work for most people. They don't like that kind of instruction from others, because in the end they wind up feeling like they don't communicate well with their boss. They feel like you just don't care and you don't really want it to be done thoroughly.

And yet, I really appreciate those people who take the time to focus and listen to what you have to say. They want to make sure they get every detail written down.

They want to know if doing it one way is OK, or if another way is OK. They are thinking through this project in a nice, logical manner and they will get it done so much better than I would do, which is exactly what you want on your team.

But if you don't start well, it causes way too many problems, and *I* caused too many problems in my career. So today I try to be aware of myself and therefore, adjust to what I see other people need. Maybe you have some of that yourself.

I finally got a clear picture of my behavior when I watched an old movie. It was the modern-day version of the *Beverly Hillbillies*. There is a scene in that movie between Miss Jane and Jethro that I absolutely love!

Jethro, who is supposed to be the big dummy, wants to run an advertising campaign to find a wife for Uncle Jed. He wanted to go into Beverly Hills and have billboards, ads, and all kinds of advertising, and he told Miss Jane that. She was the brains of the show, so she's at the computer, going on and on and looking at all the metrics of what they could do – we could do these billboards and get an 8% market penetration, and if we do this and run a full page ad we get another 28%. She was going on and on with all these metrics and Jethro is looking at her dumbfounded, and you can tell from his expression that he is not getting it at all. He doesn't have a clue of what she's talking about.

Jethro just looks at her and says, "Miss Jane, I don't understand the words coming out of your mouth."

Oh, my, gosh! That is me to a 'T.' I would think I was expressing what needed to be done, and I thought in my own mind I was clear, I'd been thorough, and that I'd given people the information they needed. Yet when I'd look at them I could see a person looking back at me like Jethro did. It was like they could see my mouth moving, they hear words coming out of my mouth, but it's obvious that what I was saying didn't mean a thing.

Maybe you have had that same type of experience. If you have, then this is your clue that you need to improve. It's not their problem. It's *our* problem, because it is *our* responsibility to make sure the job gets done. So if it is *our* responsibility to get the job done, then what we've got to do is get better.

Here are some things that you can do to get better.

1) Begin to think about the specifics of what needs to be done, and then plan those specifics.

We don't tend to stop, think and plan, so I encourage you to do that, and to do it well. When you do it well, the benefit is that your people begin to feel empowered. Being empowered means that they are confident they clearly understood what you said needed to be done and they are more than willing to go tackle the project. They've got a clear picture. It's nothing more than painting the picture or giving them the movie in their mind. You tell them what scenes come next. What needs to be done? What's it going to look like when you get to the conclusion of the movie?

When you do that, people really feel empowered, and they'll do their job in a much more effective way.

2) Another thing we should do more effectively is express deadlines, give the proper authority and provide additional

details that usually come after that initial discussion. Likely we've all experienced the situation when we thought we gave really good instructions. Yet, once the person began working on the project, they would come back over and over asking additional questions.

When people are coming back to you with lots of interim project questions that is your clue to listen and improve the next time. Start making a list of those things that people tend to come back to you for more often. What you'll begin to see is a clear picture of the steps that you tend to leave out.

Many people do well by creating a checklist of things they need to share with other people, no matter what the project is. They'll have a blank checklist to remind them of what they often forget to tell people. For myself, I found that people were coming back to ask for additional authority, so I've got that specifically identified now.

I tell them exactly what the budget is and if they go over I need them to come back and get authorization. If they need to go over 1% or 2%, that's OK. In other words, you've got to be that specific. You've got to help people understand exactly what those details need to be in order for them to feel empowered.

You also want to make sure to detail exactly how you want them to handle roadblocks. Sometimes when roadblocks come up, people will just stop. They'll stop dead in the middle, and won't do anything. They won't even come and talk to you. That's why it would be a good idea, as part of your giving directions, to mention that if they experience a roadblock, to come back to you. Don't wait, come to you immediately. The better you get the more you can anticipate the type of roadblocks that are going to come up. If you do anticipate those specific things being a roadblock, you can head them off ahead of time and get roadblocks removed before they become an issue.

That's another step in the direction process. You want to avoid doing the work yourself because you want your team to grow. You want your individual employees to grow. You want them and the process to work effectively. If you're doing a lot of the work yourself, just like you did when you were an individual contributor, you create a demotivating environment for the whole team. You're defeating the effort of the team. They are more than willing to let you do all of the work if that is what you want to do.

You wind up doing the work, and you do too much. You don't have any time to breathe. Great managers understand that planning, preparation, and delegation are skills developed over time. We each can get better at these types of things.

But it starts with planning and thinking about the details that need to be done.

In summary, review past projects that you've had. Really think about what went wrong, what you were not clear about and look for patterns. Consider setting up ways to benchmark your improvement, just like the checklist I mentioned above. Create your own checklist so you can make sure that you are giving clear directions and helping your team.

Be committed to doing this. It doesn't happen just by thinking or reading about it. You've got to commit yourself to it. Set yourself up for success.

Another great way to improve is to ask team members if you are giving them enough information. What would have helped you do this project better and faster? What else could you have given that could have helped them?

There are a lot of benefits to that. You'll not only give better information the next time, but you are also showing your team that you are committed to continual improvement yourself. Not just them, but you, too. You're not afraid to change, you embrace their interaction, and you want to be able to get better too.

Often times when we are giving directions a manager will forget to include the reasons why something needs to be done and then neglect to mention the timeframe that it needs to be done in. They tend to imply 'just do it because I said to do it, because I'm your boss.' All that does is create friction and it doesn't motivate people. It actually de-motivates them and they really need to own the reason. They need to understand it.

We humans love knowing the reason why we're doing something. If we understand the reason something needs to be done, we can buy into that and understand why there is a sense of urgency. We can then do our work better.

CHAPTER FOUR

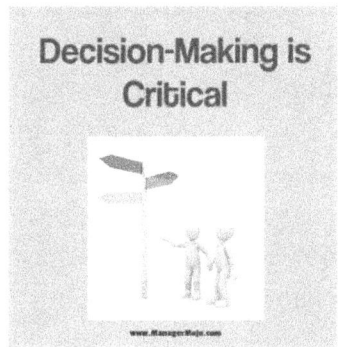

Decision-Making is
Critical

www.ManagerMojo.com

YOU CAN'T MAKE A DECISION

The ability to make decisions in a timely and effective manner is a very important skill for every manager to develop. Yet, it's one of those skill sets that many struggle with. They don't understand the real importance of making timely decisions.

First let's talk about what decision making is. As a manager, you are continually faced with your direct reports asking for input on various matters. Sometimes they just want your idea and opinion, but sometimes they want you to decide on the proper direction they should take. They are looking for you to tell them exactly what they should do on a project.

Most of us struggle with decisions for ourselves. We tend to avoid decisions in our own personal life, so when we come to work we already have a bias against making that quick decision. The problem is that we may take too long to make a decision or we don't appear to be willing to offer our opinion and make a decision.

Yet, you must master this as a manager, because you're going to be asked to decide which players should be on your team. Which people you should spend time with. You need to determine what skills need to be developed for each team member. So, it is up to you to make these decisions along the way. It is important for you to be adept and good at decision making.

Maybe it might help to understand this topic if I talk about what poor decision-making looks like. I'll give you one that I've seen and experienced personally.

Early in my career, I had a manager who called a meeting and asked everyone to give their opinion about a particular direction that he wanted to go. We were all encouraged before the meeting to think about the advantages and disadvantages of this direction. It was presented as a 'let's discuss this' type of meeting.

We go into the meeting and this individual starts by asking for feedback. We began to give our opinions, and as soon as we gave our opinion the manager would push back. He'd try to shoot down what our arguments were. It didn't take much time of watching other people get criticized for their opinion that our antennae went up and my co-workers and I wondered what we were really doing.

And then out of the blue, the manager states, 'OK, I've just decided to do this.' Well, what was the point of having the meeting? Why ask for everyone's opinion and then undermine people whenever they gave an opinion different from the direction he had already decided? Why not communicate that decision and make it a different type of meeting? It should have been a different type of communication.

That's decision making where someone had already made a decision, but it was so poorly communicated that all it did was create push-back, arguments and de-energize the entire group.

That's just one type of experience. Another example is of the employee who has to go to their manager for an approval. They are asked to make a decision because there is a deadline, and the employee needs their guidance on what to do. But the manager says, 'Let me get back to you. I need to think about that and do some research.' That seems appropriate, so you go off to do other work.

Yet, the manager never comes back to let you know if he's made a decision. Of course, you go back to inquire, and he again says that he needs to think about it, look into it, and make a couple of phone calls. So you remind him of the deadline that is approaching.

You wait patiently for the manager. And if you've ever been in that boat you know it's not a fun position to be in, because you want to get this project complete, but you can't get an answer from your boss.

Unfortunately, if you're wired like I am you're not very patient. You want to get that decision made and get that project complete.

Well, what happens at that point? You go back to the manager, and now the manager is losing patience because you're pushing them to make a decision that frankly they should have made to begin with. You shouldn't have to push a manager to make a decision. The fact was it ruined all of that individual's credibility with their team members because they were continually holding up the entire team.

Those are just two examples of poor decision making that drives your employees crazy. It is a huge de-motivator on teams.

Another reason people are so poor at decision making is because they understand that risk is involved. They know that they can be criticized for making a wrong decision. Let's be clear right now, that is the first thing you've got to get over as a manager.

You are going to have to take some risks. You're going to have to be willing to take some criticism for decisions that are not perfect. Everybody can make perfect decisions by looking in the rear-view mirror, so you must understand that criticism comes with the process.

In "decision-making 101" there are 7 steps, and I'm going to share with you my 7 step process for making decisions.

1) Understand the risk.

You need to look at every decision and determine what the risks are to the organization. Take yourself personally out of the equation. You need to think not just about your career but you need to think about the team members. Understand the risk involved in the decision. Some decisions can be made with practically no risk at all. Make them quickly and move on. The fact is, when you have complex decisions, if you study the situation and you understand the risk, you will nearly always make the right decision. There is nothing that says you can't ask for input from other people.

2) Be clear on what you are deciding.

It is reality that far too often we are distracted and we fail to hear questions or statements properly. When we're distracted, we think we've heard what the decision we need to make is, but we don't, and we end up making the decision on the wrong question. In other words, we didn't really understand the situation we were being asked to decide upon.

So be clear about what you are deciding on. If you don't understand on what you are deciding, ask questions immediately. Your team members will absolutely respect the fact that you took the time to ask questions about this decision. Get all of that information so that it helps you understand the risk.

Be very clear about what you are deciding on.

3) Determine if this is a multiple step decision tree.

If this is a complex decision, it might require you to ask for the opinions of others before you make the decision. You need to determine quickly who you should ask and why you are going to be asking for their opinion. Often we delay decisions because we think we need to go ask someone else. But the question you should be asking yourself is, do you really?

In other words, do I already have the experience I need to make this decision myself? Many people will make decisions quickly and others delay. They want to get all of the facts. They want to get everyone's opinion, develop consensus, and by the time this happens often the decision is never made and the project is lost. So, if it is a multiple-step decision tree, then get a plan to do it but get it fast. You need to move through it.

Often managers know they could ask for other's opinions, but they also know what everyone is going to say, so they move on to decide it themselves. If it turns out wrong, they'll ask for forgiveness later. They turn out to be more effective managers and certainly develop into better leaders primarily because they are willing to take risks. They are willing to cut out the decision trees. They are willing to prune them so that they only go to get those additional opinions when necessary.

4) Anticipate roadblocks ahead.

When you make a decision, since you're the manager and the leader, you need to anticipate the roadblocks that your team is going to face if you make a decision in a certain way. By anticipating these road-blocks, you can give permission to move forward at a faster pace. This helps your team be more effective.

You don't want to be a manager that says every decision has got to come back to you. Therefore, that requires you to anticipate roadblocks so that you can effectively work with your team.

And that leads directly into the fifth step.

5) Decide how much authority you're going to delegate.

When you make good decisions you also learn how to delegate real authority. So many managers are afraid to delegate real authority.

When I created my first business we were very small and every dollar counted. I needed to get some manuals copied, and I needed about 20 of them. I had an assistant who was young and she didn't understand much about her role. I had not trained her properly. It was one of those things where I was moving fast and I made a lot of assumptions.

I told her I needed to get the manuals copied, how many I needed, and I let her decide how she was going to go about getting that done. Well, I thought what she would do is take them to a printer and get them copied and bound. That doesn't cost very much money. But what she did instead was go to the nearest place and make actual copies. She did exactly what I'd asked her to do. She gave me the copies of the manuals, but instead of a project costing maybe $400-500, she brought back a bill of $2,000.

I was shocked and asked her what she did. Well, she went to one of the local places and paid the higher cost per page to get this thing printed and copied. She took me literally that I actually wanted copies.

I understood very quickly the value of delegating real authority and also risk. But you know what, it was OK, because she got a project done, and she got it done in a hurry. That's the point here. The cool thing is that over a period of time, because of that example, it made her a much more effective team contributor. Instead of blindly doing something, she would ask questions and helped to train me as well.

Decide how much authority to delegate.

6) Set up a review process.

You should always review the progress of projects within your team. You need to be able to set the expectations that you are going to be involved and how you are going to be involved. What you are doing here is making yourself available as a resource. You're saying, 'OK team, I made the decision, let's go,' but you're not looking over their shoulder every second, deciding at every point what needs to be done. That slows things down, and yet most managers don't understand that they can set a review process.

Now, the next and final step is, in my opinion, the most important, once you've gone through all the prior thought.

7) Determine your communication plan for the decision.

We don't often understand how to communicate properly with our team members, so we don't give them all of our thoughts. We get in a hurry, we give piecemeal thoughts, and we don't communicate well. It goes back to my earlier example where the manager wanted input but he didn't really want input because he had already made his decision. If you've already made a decision, why not communicate that decision, give your team members all the reasons and move on. It saves everyone a lot of time, and everyone knows what their marching orders are.

When you don't develop a communication plan you appear to be wishy-washy in your decision making. It appears that you are a person that doesn't make firm decisions. This is a de-motivator for your team and for you as a leader, because it causes you to lose respect from your team members. They are always questioning if you're sure about your decisions. They wonder if you're going to come back to them and reprimand them for doing something wrong. They can smell wishy-washy.

You want their respect, and that means you need to make good decisions. You need to make them firmly and you've got to communicate decisions clearly to your team members.

A poor communication plan lowers team performance, and you want to avoid that.

Show me a poor team, and I'll show you an indecisive leader. They don't ever know what to do next. So they do a little bit and they stop and wait for directions. They do a little bit more, stop, and they wait for directions. And they do that again. You get the idea. Everything has to be given permission and blessings. That is not decision making, that's simply being a dictator. And it doesn't work. It kills your team performance.

So, learn how to make decisions that include other people and empower them to get the job done. You will then be looked at as a much more effective and better leader.

Let's summarize, because we've talked about quite a few things.

Decision making doesn't need to be hard, but it needs to be done. You've got to be able to communicate why you made a decision. That's the last thing I want to talk about.

When you communicate the reasons behind the decision that you made, that is incredibly empowering to your team. Whenever they receive pushback from others inside or outside the company they can explain the reasons why the company wants it this way. They can clearly communicate, and they don't have to bring you in the middle of it. They've already got your opinion and know what your thoughts are.

You not only need to communicate the decision you made, but communicate the reasons why you made the decision. That allows your team members to understand what the parameters are when there comes a time that you're not available and they need to make a decision. They need to feel comfortable in doing that. But if you've never explained the reason why you made certain decisions then they can't anticipate that; therefore, you don't take advantage of the full skill sets of your team and you're not developing them as you should.

So "decision-making 101" means make decisions, and make them effectively. Think about those 7 steps, understand the risk, be clear about what you're deciding on, determine what the decision tree is, anticipate and ask the opinions of others, think about the roadblocks, decide how much authority you're really going to delegate, set up a review process and in your communications plan be clear about the decision as well as the reasons for that decision.

CHAPTER FIVE

I trust the people who are working with me. I delegate.

Mario Draghi

www.ManagerMojo.com

YOU REFUSE TO DELEGATE

In my mind, delegation is one of the most important skills you must master as a manager and a leader. If you want to maximize and increase your mojo, then you need to understand what delegation is, how to master it and how to use it to leverage your talents and skills. That's when you'll be off and running to a successful career and you'll be the respected leader and manager that you want to be.

First, let's define delegation. Delegation is the art of assigning tasks and responsibilities to team members in order to maximize their talent, skills and ability. It is the ability to assign effectively.

The problem is that most managers struggle with delegation, especially those who have a desire to control everything going on around them. Delegation can be the skill that derails your career and derails the progress of their team. In fact, over the years what I've seen is that most managers struggle with delegation.

The reason they struggle is varied. Let me review a few of them.

One of the reasons that managers can struggle with delegation is because they don't trust other people. This idea of trust and delegation go hand in hand, because you should be able to trust that somebody else can do a job as quickly and as well as you. The problem is that this is not natural.

For those of us who have been around a while, we know that not everybody does things the same way that we would do them. Maybe they don't do it to the same quality or level that you do them.

Let me give you an example of where delegation can hold you back. I've watched this so many times.

I had a friend that had a successful business. He was growing his business but his business was a lot about his own ideas, his own talent and the ability to get stuff done. He kept getting more and more clients because the fact was he was good at what he was doing and people enjoyed working with him.

He decided that because his business was growing, he was going to hire somebody to help. So he did, but he didn't spend a lot of time training the person. He didn't spend a lot of time getting to know them and their strengths. He would assign a task, and when it didn't get done the way he wanted it done, he began to think the person just couldn't do it as well.

He began to get more and more involved, and he started doing the same tasks that he had delegated. Before long he was doing what he was doing before. He was working himself to death, not getting any real help. He decided that delegation wasn't working for him, that other people couldn't do what he did, and they wouldn't do it to the level he did. No matter who he hired and no matter who he gave tasks to they just didn't do them as well.

You can see where this is leading, and it led to the point where he just finally gave up on delegation and went back to doing everything himself. Of course, he topped his business growth right there.

This was a decision that I believe was the wrong decision. But here he is some 25 years later, and he's still managing that business the same way, and he can't grow because he doesn't trust anyone to do something as well as he does. He cannot delegate it. This happens far too often.

I can hear you saying, 'Yeah Steve, I know all that stuff. I know that I need to delegate. That's a good story, but why don't you tell me something that I don't know?'

OK, let's talk about that. Let me give you the example of my first good manager.

That first manager happened to be my Mom. You see, my Mom worked outside the house. It was up to my brother and me to clean the house for her. She assigned cleaning chores for us to do. She delegated these responsibilities.

Well, mine was to clean the floors, to do the vacuuming and to clean the bathroom. I remember when she assigned vacuuming. She was very meticulous. She would show me what to do and how I should run the vacuum. She showed me the best way to get all the dirt and dust off, and then she showed me exactly how I was to do the vacuuming, and how I was supposed to do the mopping so that the floors looked good.

The cool thing about this is that once she assigned it to me she didn't stand over me and watch me do it. She let me go ahead and clean the floors. I did what I thought was good, and then she came and reviewed my progress.

Well, when she reviewed my progress she said, "Steve, you did a really good job here on your first effort. It's not bad at all. You've done a lot of things well, but let me show you a few things that you missed because you haven't had the experience."

She showed me how I should pick up the rugs and shake them out first before vacuuming, and to vacuum around them.

What I had done was vacuum the rugs on the floor and when you pulled up the rug there was dirt around where the rug laid on the floor. And I remember thinking, 'Oh, so that's how you do it!' She reviewed it, but she didn't criticize me. She just said this is something else you ought to do that will make the floors look even better and they'll be easier to clean. She was absolutely right. She was showing me exactly what needed to be done.

The cool thing is that not only did she teach me how to do it, she reinforced that I was doing it well. She did the exact same things with the bathroom, and I learned how to clean a bathroom and make it spotless because she reviewed my work.

She delegated it and let me go off on my own and do it. Then she reviewed my work and pointed out ways that I could do it better. Once I began to do it better, this is where the magic happened. Did she just take for granted that I was going to do it well? No, every time she came in after I'd done the vacuuming and bathroom, she would review my work. She'd walk around, look at it, and she'd then say, "Steve, that is a great job. You are doing terrific!" She reinforced that doing it well meant something to her and it meant something to others.

Yes, that's delegation. The additional plus is that those lessons where you do things well and it's been reinforced that you were doing them well become life-long habits. I can assure you that through my entire life my family has been blessed by the fact that I can vacuum and I can clean a bathroom. I don't mind at all. The reason I don't mind is because I think it's cool to look at it after it's done. I get that same feeling of contentment and joy that my Mom gave me by doing a job well.

When I began to go to work for other people and I began to manage other people, those lessons reminded me that all of us need that reinforcement. We need to be taught first, and we need the reinforcement that we're doing well. That's when delegation begins to develop trust. Mom began to trust me because I was doing it well consistently, and it was very important for me to continue to earn her trust because I knew that she was paying attention.

That's pretty cool, and it's a great lesson. If you don't get anything else out of this program and you get that, you begin to realize that you can do this with your people too.

But some of you find it difficult to trust others. You're risk averse and you don't like taking chances. The problem is that you don't trust *yourself* completely, so learn to develop trust in yourself.

The second step to changing your delegation skills is to manage *yourself*. You need to dig in to your own strengths. If you haven't written down what things you are great at, you need to take a moment right now to make that list. I promise you, there are things that you're really outstanding at. It could be that you're a great communicator. It could be that you have great analytical skills. It could be that you have great vision. These things are strengths. You need to write them down, and put them where you can read them. Regularly remind yourself of what you are great at.

Begin to read this list out loud to yourself. By reading those strengths out loud you will begin to trust yourself. You'll begin to learn how to manage yourself and your actions to your strengths. This is how you learn to leverage your strengths and how you learn to become a good teacher.

You see, managers and leaders, at their core, are outstanding teachers. You've got to be willing to tolerate mistakes. Let me give you an example.

Good teachers do several things, and let me tell you the steps that they follow.

First is that they teach. They share material that the student has not learned before.

The second thing they do is assign tasks that reinforce the teaching. It could be homework, exercises or problems. They assign those tasks and let the students attempt those problems and tasks on their own. They test or review the answers that the students have made to make sure they got the information.

A manager who wants to have maximum mojo and be their best must follow that exact same process. You as a manager have got to be willing to teach your employee what you want to be done when you delegate. Give complete directions, instruct them on those areas that they don't know, and then delegate the task. Assign time frames. Delegate it, and when it's done review it. If there are mistakes, it's OK. You need to build up your team. You need to tell them, 'That was a great first effort! Here's an area I think we might have missed. Let's add it. Let's complete it. Awesome job! I'm so glad you do that!'

You see, when you learn how to do that, things become more fun. If it's difficult for you to do this type of thing, let me recommend that you start with easy tasks and keep adding things until you get better. But you need to be willing to start with the tasks that make you feel good. When you begin to realize that people can do stuff, it will begin to allow you some freedom and flexibility that you haven't had before.

As I suggested a moment ago of writing down your personal strengths, you should do the same thing for the members of your team. Be very aware of them – both your strengths and theirs. You should be observant of the things they do exceptionally well. You need to know those things, and you need to leverage those strengths every chance you get.

Every time you get an opportunity to assign something to somebody you're going to build your confidence and trust in them. You'll begin to feel more confident in your ability to manage.

And guess what the real benefit is. When you review tasks with the employee, you're building their confidence and their strengths. You're building their trust in you as a leader. This is how you get maximum mojo. This is how you make yourself and your career explode and grow in the direction you want it to go.

People must be willing to trust you as the leader. You can't be trusted as a leader unless you can trust your team members. You can't manage your team members unless you can manage yourself.

You should continue to do these things until they begin to feel natural and comfortable to you. The cool thing is that as you keep doing these things, before you know it you're going to be delegating not only tasks, but you're going to begin to delegate real authority that you've been given in your position to others. That's necessary for your employees to grow.

It will allow you to delegate the authority to manage the team to someone whenever you want to take vacation, or you have to be out ill. You'll begin to trust that they're going to do it well because you've seen them do it well. You've complimented them on doing it well. They've got your back, and you've got their back. Before you know it you're that dynamic leader that every person in the organization wants to work with because you value them and you value yourself.

You can't fake valuing other people unless you value yourself. Faking it doesn't work. I've heard so many people say, 'Fake it until you make it.' Well, I've got to tell you that is one way to walk forward when you're in fear, but when it comes to human beings you must value them by trusting them and you've got to trust yourself first to do that. You can't fake that. If you don't trust yourself, it won't come across that you trust others. Nobody wins when that is happening.

I want to encourage you to master these delegation skills. Consider the stories I've shared with you. Make them your own stories and begin to challenge yourself to do better at delegation. Start today. If you do, in just a few months, a few years, you're going to look back and say, 'Wow, look at where my career is now. I'm so glad I mastered the skill of delegation, because delegation allowed me to grow in ways that I could never have imagined.'

CHAPTER SIX

YOU THINK I SHOULD MOTIVATE MYSELF

This topic is very personal to me, because, you see, it's all about expectations.

It's the expectations you have first and foremost with yourself, not others. Yet I'll admit to you, when I first started in management I believed it was the expectations of *my employees* that I had to pay the most attention to. And you know what, I was just plain wrong!

Let me share by giving you an idea of the mindset I had when I first discovered the difference.

I grew up in a rural area of the country. We didn't have much. As a matter of fact, I didn't have much at all. But I didn't know that. I didn't really think about it. What I did know is that I believed in hard work. I believed that if you worked hard you could get anything that you wanted. Even though I didn't have much, just the minimum, I knew that I would have to earn everything that I ever got in life.

I mean, that's a great message. However, I think I probably took it to the extreme. You see, I'd get up early and I'd arrive at work early and stay late. That's the way I've always worked. I would get to work early, work like a demon, and work until it was late. I was always one of the first to arrive and one of the last to leave.

You know the guy. I believed you had to give everything you had because you were there to earn money. You were there to earn your paycheck. And make no mistake, I wanted to earn money and I knew that the harder I worked the better that I would do.

I could easily observe that other people had things that I didn't have. I wasn't jealous, but what I assumed was that they were smarter than I was and that somehow they had gotten ahead of me.

Also, I was extremely competitive and I still am today. I wanted to win the game of life, the game of making money, the game of having what I wanted in my life. So, I was totally all in.

So far that sounds OK, doesn't it? I mean who wouldn't want to have a competitive, hard worker that's willing to give 100% of their effort? It's a great thing. Those beliefs are good. They are healthy, and they are great beliefs to live by.

But there's a major flaw lurking in the dark. It's hiding and waiting to come out, waiting to bite you. It was going to bite *me*. It wasn't until much later that I figured out exactly what it was.

I continued working hard and doing all those things that I needed to do. I worked hard at school, I worked hard at sports, I worked hard in the jobs I had. Those jobs started when I was 13 years old. Back then, it was just fine for you to work at 13 years of age for somebody else. I worked in a small country store.

Everyday I'd get off the school bus and work until 6:00 at night. I'd go in Saturday at 7:00 a.m. and work until 6:00 that night. I had fun. My job was to pump gas, sell groceries, and load feed bags that weighed almost as much as I did into the cars and trucks of our customers. I absolutely loved it!

Although I wasn't getting much money, (as a matter of fact I still remember, I made $13.65 for an entire week of work), it was more than I had (which was nothing) and the cool thing is that I was getting feedback for my great attitude and hard work from my boss. I was saving money. I felt like I was on top of the world. I have always had a job from that time on.

I graduated to better and better jobs and I learned more and more about how to be successful. Well, the common denominator was that I was the type of person that was never going to let you out-work me. That just wasn't going to happen. I would out-work you, and I would win! I did it in sports and I did it in work.

The simple fact was that I loved to work. I truly did. I was a workaholic, and I suppose by some people's definition I still am.

Now, how long do you think it was that my hard work got me noticed and drew attention for my first management job? You're right, just like yourself, it wasn't long. It wasn't long at all. I'm certain that's exactly how you became a manager and how you became a leader. You worked just as hard as I did. You worked your tail off and you did everything that you had to do to be successful. You had a great attitude. You came early and you stayed late. In other words, what you were doing was the same thing I was doing. You earned your stripes, so to speak.

Well, so far there is absolutely nothing wrong here, right? I mean, absolutely nothing. It's great to be a hard worker, a competitor, a person of standards, a person who is willing to arrive early and stay late and get the job done. I'd get it done but get it done with quality.

What do you think happened to me when I got promoted to that first manager job?

This was the thing that was lurking in the dark that was going to bite me.

You see, (and this is my honest thinking here) I thought that everybody thought the same way that I did. That was the flaw. I made an assumption that was far from the truth and far from the norm.

The clear majority of people are not work-aholics. They work to live. I lived to work. There was a huge difference there. That difference can and does play out many different ways at work. I brought the bag-gage of unrealistic expectations with me to the job.

Make a note of that – don't bring unrealistic expectations to the job. In my brain, I truly expected other people to do what I did, to think like I thought. I thought they would emulate my work ethic. I thought they would look at me and say, 'Man, I want to work just as hard as Steve. I want to keep up with that dude.' It just made no sense to me that others could think differently. I just didn't get it.

Those who didn't try to match my standards and my expectations I assumed were just lazy.

The fact was, I was wrong, wrong, wrong. Those people weren't lazy. The problem was that I had ridiculous expectations for other people, and I didn't have the right to put my expectations on somebody else.

You can only control yourself. You can only expect things from yourself. So I had to learn how to manage people that had expectations different from my own. I had to learn that they did the job differently than I did.

That was not easy for me. It was difficult to let go of that, because I continually fought my expectations and I fought the urge to get in there and tell them what to do. I had to learn that they had the right to live their life the way they wanted to.

For a long period all I wanted to do when people weren't listening to what I had to say, meeting my expectations, or working as hard as I was, I wanted to scream, "You came to work, now EARN it!"

In my mind, 'earn it' meant something – like a crazy guy – to go way above and beyond what the job required. The fact was what I meant when I said that was I wanted them to earn it *my* way. Don't just come to work and earn your paycheck, earn your paycheck *my* way. Their way wasn't as good as mine. At least, I thought it wasn't.

At first, I took the easy way out. I just dictated. I told people what I wanted them to do, and I irritated people to get it done the way that I expected. Thankfully, it didn't take me long to see that I was getting nowhere with this attitude. It is easy to see you're not getting anywhere when people begin to ignore you and they begin to think you're a pain in their side. I mean, yes, I got the message quickly.

But, let me ask you a question. Maybe you haven't had such an extreme situation, but this is a valid question for you and those people you may be having trouble dealing with. Whose responsibility was it to change? Well, I hope you said it was *your* responsibility, because the right answer is that it is always *our* responsibility to change. Not them. I can't change them. I can only change *me*.

I had to let go of the expectations I had of others. I had to understand that I couldn't expect people to be someone different at work than who they were. If they were trying to be like me they weren't being themselves. Do you understand that? When people are trying to do what you tell them to do, what you order them to do and what you expect them to do it is so far away from what they normally believe and what they normally will do, guess what? It's not going to work.

Over time they are going to reject your leadership. They are going to reject your opinion. Give them long enough, they are going to quit you and leave the company because they just can't take you anymore.

That began the process of me understanding how to value the differences in other people, and more importantly even if I could see those differences, I learned that I had to *value* their opinion and *value* their skills, talent and work ethic as much as I valued my own. That was a big eye opening experience.

I began to learn that people were coming to work to earn their paycheck. They were simply doing it differently than I was. I began to learn that their ways were as good as mine and sometimes better because they did it faster and more accurately than I would have done.

But for a long period I still privately thought that my way was better. So, my subliminal communication was bad. Thankfully over a period of time, when you're really working on something, working to value other people and wanting to do better, you begin to be better.

My expectations changed. I began to learn to delegate and let them decide. My expectations began to line up more with the goals of the job rather than the goals of Steve. You see, there's a huge difference between what the goals of the job are and what you personally have for your own goals.

If you've ever been in sales, you know exactly what I'm talking about. In sales, your management team will give you a goal and an objective that you must meet to earn your paycheck and keep your job or to get bonuses. For me, when I got those kinds of goals those were not *my* goals. That was a minimum level of performance to me. My goals were always way higher than what my bosses gave me. It just didn't make sense to me to try to do the minimum. I wasn't there to keep my job; I was there to be outstanding. I expected myself to do it.

Other people are not going to have that kind of competitiveness, and they aren't going to have that kind of commitment, nor should they. It isn't necessary to have a great life.

I began to understand that the fact was that I had to let this stuff go. I began to see how my own expectations for other people were holding them back from the success they wanted, and more importantly I was holding them back from them being their best. T*he only way somebody can be their best is if you encourage them to be their best person, have their best ideas, and let them grow to whatever level they need to grow to.* Don't put your expectations on someone else.

This is not an easy lesson. It requires something every day that you must work on.

Beginning today, I want to encourage you to do some self-examination of yourself, just like I did. Examine how your own personal expectations are spilling over into your expectations of your employees.

If you're being honest with yourself, you're going to see some disconnect. When you do see those disconnects, don't beat yourself up. Examine how you can learn from them and see if there's a way that you can let it go.

There's a minimum level we must hold people accountable to that the job requires. But what we should do is learn to allow other people to have different expectations from ours if we did that job ourselves. That's the key. We've got to let them be themselves. Let them grow at the pace that they want to grow and I promise you'll grow right along with them.

So, learn to adjust your expectations to let them be their own person.

Once you conquer this, the great news is that you can then begin to leverage the power of motivation and inspiration of other people. Because you see, you actually are meeting them from where they are. And when you meet people where they are it's much easier to motivate them to go one step further, and one step further, and one step further.

And it is much easier to inspire them by letting them see the success of that one step further than they thought they could get, and then one step further then they thought they could get. When you begin to do that and you learn that it is OK that their expectations are not where yours would have been in that job, and you just help them move one step ahead, great things begin to happen.

In my career I've seen people do so much better than where they were, but I didn't try to force them to get where I thought they should be. I let them go at their own pace and I used the power of motivation, meaning positive reinforcement, when they did stuff well, to help them be inspired to make another effort to go to another level that they didn't think they could get to.

So many people come to work and all they've heard in life is negative, negative, negative. Initially in my career that's what I was doing. I was throwing one more negative expectation on top of them. People rebel against that, and they never perform at their best.

When you learn to handle your expectations, it will change the dynamics of the relationship. When you understand this, from their perspective it will be, 'Wow! He or she is all about me, me, me!' You are now focused on *their* progress and growth, and that allows you to use the power of motivation and inspiration.

The good news is that everybody can do this. You can do it. I know I did it, and if I could do it, I know that you can too.

I have learned that my own personal expectations of myself are OK, as long as I'm not forcing them on somebody else. It's just perfectly OK to have my expectations of myself. I also learned that it's OK for other people to think differently than I do. It's just fine. It's the way they are going to be the very best they can be.

By understanding this, I learned that I could focus on the job and not me. When you can begin to focus on the goals of the job and not yourself, that's a good perspective for a successful manager and leader to have. It allows each one of us to earn our way in the world. I can earn my way with my expectations, and you can earn your way based on your expectations. That's when it becomes an enjoyable and enlightening experience for both of us.

CHAPTER SEVEN

Be the coach to your team
www.ManagerMojo.com

MY BOSS DOESN'T COACH ME, SO WHY SHOULD I COACH YOU?

I want to share a few things that I hope will help you understand how you can coach and improve the performance of your team.

It has been my experience that 9 out of 10 managers never invest time in coaching their direct reports. That is a staggering thought, but I can just tell you that very few people will invest the time. They understand that if you're going to coach people, it takes time.

Let me talk about what coaching is and how I'm defining it. That way it will help you. A lot of people will say they coach people. They talk with their team members all the time, and they consider that coaching. But that isn't coaching. That is managing the process and managing what they do, when they do it, and how they do it.

The simple definition of coaching is **the teaching of your direct reports the things they need to do and they need to know, in order to do their job successfully**.

Frankly, if most of us did that simple definition alone, we would have more productive employees and less disengagement in the workplace. Sadly, most of us hardly do that. What we do is tell them what their job is, point them to the resources available, and then we depend on them to figure it out on their own.

I must tell you, this is something that was hard for me to learn, and it shouldn't have been. In my own life, back when I was in high school, I worked for a wonderful man that was a real estate appraiser. He was an amazing manager, but I didn't understand it at the time. I was too young and too inexperienced to understand what a great manager he was.

He taught me all about appraising real estate. The thing that was so cool is that he'd ask me to do things like drawing the outline of a house or a piece of property, and doing it to scale. He'd explain why we were doing those things. He'd not only show me how to do it, but he explained the reasons why we were doing things.

When we started doing research for comparable properties to determine whether we could put an equal, greater or lower value on that piece of property, he would explain what he was doing, how he was doing it, and what we were looking for. Basically, what he was doing was teaching me everything that I needed to know to not only do the work but also to understand the work.

The fact is I got good at that. Even in high school he gave me a piece of property after a few months and he said 'I want you to do this one all on your own and see what you come back with.' So I did. I did it all on my own, and I came back with what I thought was the recommended value of the property.

He reviewed it and concurred. Sure enough, that property sold for exactly what we had appraised it for.

He used to tell people what a great job I had done; he was demonstrating great coaching. He was demonstrating teaching of everything. But I must tell you, I didn't get it at all. It went over my head, because when I got to the corporate world after graduating from college, and I started going to work, it wasn't that way.

What happened is that I did a job. They'd tell me here's your job and here is what you're supposed to do, here's what you have available. Good luck, go get it done. It was up to me to figure out what to do. I had very little interaction with any of my managers, except to see if I was meeting my goals or not.

Frankly, I accepted that as the norm. It wasn't until much later that I began to understand that other people were having the same problem I had. They couldn't figure out what they needed to do, because they got so little feedback from their boss. But by this time, I was the boss. I wasn't giving them the feedback and they weren't as effective as they needed to be.

That's when I began to understand that coaching is all about teaching everything they need to know so that they can do their job successfully.

It was tough for me to learn this, because I didn't like hand holding. That's what I called coaching. I thought it was hand holding. Maybe you feel the same way. Frankly, the problem wasn't that it was hand holding, it was that I didn't know how to do it effectively. I thought it took too much of my time, and I was always way too busy with meetings, deadlines, other employee requests, and expectations from my boss. After all, I had to figure it out for myself, too.

This 'figure it out yourself' culture of business is our inheritance. We've got it throughout the world. And it's carried out daily in companies where we expect people to figure it out.

We pay a price for that, and the price is high turnover, employees who are unmotivated, and more importantly they're totally ineffective. But it doesn't have to be that way. There is a better way.

I'm recommending that you implement coaching to take your team to the next level, and I'm going to give you some principles that you can follow so that you can understand how to do effective coaching yourself.

The first thing I want you to understand, remember and engrain in your thinking is that you cannot do it all by yourself. Now think about that. You know you can't do everything by yourself. But here's what you need to think about. If you can't do it all by yourself, then your employees can't either. They need help just as much as you do. They need direction just as much as you do.

So, you should not only teach your employees but you should also connect with your employees. The fact is you have to connect before you teach. That's what my real estate mentor was doing. He was connecting with me on my level. He reached down and he understood exactly what my issues were. He understood my confusion. He understood how to take me from confusion to understanding. When I went from confusion to understanding the next step was excellence. And it was that understanding through excellence path that made me good at appraising real estate.

I chose not to do it as a career, but I must say I really enjoyed it. It was fun because I felt like I was good at it.

Here is what I want to recommend that you do. When you're coaching and teaching, it means you must sit down with your direct report in a one-on-one environment. I can already tell that most of you are going to say 'wait a minute I don't have time to do that.' I know it takes time. But the fact is, if you're doing it well these meetings don't have to be long. They should start with maybe 20 minutes. You will be amazed, if you're organized, how much you can get done in 20 minutes. At least that would be a good start with your employees.

Here are 11 steps that you can take right now to begin to do effective coaching:

1) Start with sharing what you see and observe are the employee's top three strengths. It means you've got to invest a little time to think about what they are good at. You need to know what they are good at.

2) Ask them what their top strengths are. It may be different from what you see, and it would be cool to make sure you're on the same page. You've got to know what you consider to be their top strengths and what they consider their top three strengths. Then make sure your lists match.

3) Explain to the employee that it is by using our strengths that we can do a great job, and that individual will enjoy their work and do a great job. You see, it's not the things that we're not good at that we become successful at. The way we become successful is by doing those things that we are good at, doing them more frequently, and doing them better and better. When people are doing things they are good at they get better. That is how you increase productivity on your team, by explaining that you want them to use their strengths.

4) This step is very important, because here you're going to ask them what they see are obstacles to doing their job well. We all have obstacles, and occasionally those obstacles are going to change. But, you'll be surprised at how quickly a direct report can tell you what's keeping them from doing what they need to do and what's causing

them frustration in their job. Once you identify that obstacle, then step 5 is . . .

5) Explore ways to remove those obstacles so they can do what they want to do and what they are good at.

6) Work together to remove the obstacles. Here's where you can move to the company goal and the expectations that you have of them and the job. It is only until you get to this point that they fully get what the expectations are and they begin to tie together in their brain how they can use their strengths to meet those expectations, and hopefully exceed them. Once you've done that, you should do step 7 when you're talking about company goals and expectations.

7) Make sure to explain the rationale for the company goals and expectations. In my own example, I was talking to my real estate mentor and he explained why we had to get everything exactly right – the measurements of the property, the buildings had to be exact because we determined pricing based on the dollar per square foot, and if we were off we were going to be off in our evaluation. That valuation was important. It could keep

people from getting financing or it could cause them to borrow more money than they should have. Maybe they overpaid for that property. So, you've got to be able to explain the rationale so that the person can start agreeing and saying to themselves, 'yes, not only do I agree with these goals, I think I can achieve them, or I can over-achieve them.'

8) Once you've done this, you now can get their buy-in. What I'm talking about when I say buy-in is get their agreement that yes, that is reasonable, and yes I can do it. You see, if they don't understand the expecta-tions, goals and rationale, how can you expect them to agree with them? More importantly, if they don't agree with them, how in the world are you going to get them motivated to go after achieving those goals? Get their agreement. Help them to understand.

(I'm breaking this down into minute steps, and you can see it doesn't take a long time to start having this type of conversation. This format works well.)

9) Now that you've talked about expecta-tions and goals and you've gotten agree-ment, let's discuss your personal interaction

with them. Set communication expectations. What I mean by that is how they will
give you updates on their progress or the
lack thereof. You'll have to assess that
expectation now. Tell them that you're
going to be asking questions, and you
encourage them to be asking questions too.
You want that dialogue to go back/forth to
make sure that you're up to date on
whatever projects you're working on.

This communication expectation takes away
the fear that a lot of people have of going to
tell their boss bad news. Many times, things
get stuck. The employee knows they are
stuck, they know they have a problem, but
they are afraid to tell their boss. Nothing
gets done because they don't have communication expectations. Explain that "you
are going to celebrate their successes and if
something is wrong, it is OK. That's our job,
to fix it. We're not worried about something
that's not going well. That's all part of the
job. What we've got to do is figure out how
to get it done together."

You set that foundation of communications
by saying that you recognize not everything
will go perfectly. It will help them a lot if
you do only that. If you skipped everything

else and you talked about communications and only did that, you'd be doing more coaching than most managers. But I'm saying don't do just that. Take every step. Make sure you're good at it.

10) Next, it's up to you to define how you're going to be giving feedback. How are they doing in the job? People want to know how they are doing. They absolutely hate uncertainty. Uncertainty is the breeding ground of disengagement. When people are uncertain of where they stand with their boss and where they stand in the company, it's easy for other people to influence them and get them off track. That influence can keep them from being the best they can be.

Your job is to give them feedback. Let them know what's going well, and what's not going so well. Please don't do what so many managers do. I can't tell you how many managers said "That's what we have annual reviews for." Oh, my goodness! If you wait or think you can wait until an annual review to give somebody feedback on how they are doing and where they're going, you've missed the whole point of your job. People hate annual reviews. Why do you think they hate annual reviews? Because it is the first time in an entire year that most people have gotten any feedback from their manager on how they are doing.

The annual review should be a celebration of all the great things that someone has done all year. An annual review should never be an excuse to say they are doing poorly at the job. That's not the first time you should be telling them 'You're terrible at it, and if you don't get your act together we're not going to keep you.' That's not the purpose of an annual review. But because managers get distracted and they don't take the time to do coaching, people aren't given feedback. This is a biggie. You must give feedback, and you've got to give feedback constantly. Don't wait once a year, because it doesn't work.

11) After you've done these great things, the next thing you should do is mark a time on your calendar and theirs for your next one-on-one meeting. This is a meeting that you've got to keep. That next one-on-one may only take five minutes, but I'll tell you what, it will be very important because you will have taken time to set an appointment to talk about where they are. You'll go back through all the things listed so far in the 11

steps. And it will go faster and faster, because now you'll begin to get agreement on their strengths, and you'll begin to get agreement on goals and expectations. You'll get buy-in.

You'll have more successful coaching sessions and you'll be able to focus on exactly what the problem is so that you can remove that obstacle and move on to greater success.

Remember this; nothing gets done without your team being effective. You can't do it all by yourself. Your real job is making sure that each person is the most effective they can be, they are engaged and they are growing within the company.

If you don't master this, then this is what you should know is the result.

Research shows that people quit managers, not companies. They just get tired of working with that particular manager. They don't feel like they connect. They don't feel like their needs are being met. They don't feel like their career is moving forward. So they quit, go somewhere else, and they hope it is going to be different there.

If you do that, if you ignore it and they quit, what's going to happen is you're always left to training new people and starting all over. That means your time gets more and more scarce. Understand that without that kind of team building, you may not make it as a manager. If your turnover gets too high, then your job will be in jeopardy. That doesn't have to happen. Proper coaching will let you always know where everybody stands. You'll know who is in jeopardy of leaving and who is not.

If you master those 11 steps, the art of coaching, teaching and connection there are three additional things you're going to get as a benefit:

1) You're going to be building trust with your team every day. That's huge. You want to build trust.

2) You're going to see an increase in performance. You'll see people doing a little better, and a little better and a little better. It is a great thing when you can see people improving.

3) You're going to be able to meet your goals and your team's goals because now

you've got everybody pulling together. It's worth the effort of being a coach.

Once you have that great communication established with your team, you'll be able to take your coaching to an entirely new level by exploring each individual's personal goals as well as their professional goals. You'll be having that communication with them, and you're becoming qualified to have that conversation.

That's when coaching becomes awesome! You're changing the direction of people's lives and careers. It's what I call the ultimate **Manager Mojo High**. It's like 'WOW!' to be able to help someone and to know that you're meeting your goals, they're helping you and you're helping them. It is a win/win for everybody!

BONUS CHAPTERS

CHAPTER EIGHT

How are you going to listen?

www.ManagerMojo.com

IF YOU WOULD LISTEN, I COULD FIX YOU

Can't you just hear managers saying that? Maybe you've said it yourself. I know I certainly have. Let's discuss the impact of statements like this, what it means and how this type of error in our thinking can get in the way of our personal and team goals.

But first I want to tell you a funny story I heard about a boss. This guy had created a task force and, if the company had a problem, he wanted them to find a solution to the problem. He charged the task force with that duty, and after they came back with their report he overrode their decision. Here's what he told them. "I'm sorry if I ever gave you the impression your input would have any effect on my decision for the outcome of this project."

Now isn't that funny and sad?!

The fact is, managers do this all the time. Unfortunately, I see managers with this type of thought process everywhere I go, and it is painful for me to watch. The reason it is painful is because it is really personal to me.

You see, I'll admit I was absolutely guilty of this when I first started managing. Maybe I didn't understand. You know, there's an old statement that says, "You don't know what you don't know." Well, I did not know what I didn't know.

Here's the way it went for me. Maybe you've felt the same way.

I honestly thought that everyone was as ambitious as I was. I thought they were driven to achieve their goals. I certainly was, and I thought every person was as driven as I was. I couldn't imagine being any different.

I also thought that everybody had to be just as proactive as I was, meaning that you're willing to get stuff done. I'm not a procrastinator. My wife, Cindy, won't tell me something that needs to be done if she thinks it might interfere with what I'm doing at that moment, because I'd get up and do it right then. I have such a drive that if somebody needs it done, I do it. I'm incredibly proactive and it is to the detriment of my own productivity at times.

I thought everyone was that proactive. I also believed that you just couldn't waste time. I understood that time's all we have. Each one of us starts every day with the same 24-hour period, and we shouldn't waste it. I thought everyone had that same sense of urgency regarding time.

I also had a deep respect for authority. I thought if someone was in charge of a company or department, if they had that title of 'boss' or 'manager,' that the position earned them respect. I showed that respect.

I would also listen intently. I would listen to the boss so that I could do what I needed to do.

Maybe you're like I was. Have you had some of the same thoughts?

The fact is, for a long time I thought the reason that some of my employees were having problems or difficulties was because they weren't listening to me. I would tell them, 'Hey, just be like me. Be proactive. Get stuff done. Take a chance. Go out and do those things.'

I would tell them that if they would do things my way, all would be well and we'd meet our goals. I was sincere about it. I was confident that was right.

But you know what? It wasn't working for me. I wasn't getting the results I wanted.

What was I missing?

Here's the key, and I hope you'll make a note of it so that you don't go as long as I did trying to figure this out. The key that I was missing is that **the way people solve problems is they draw from their own**

personal experience and their own personal internal strengths.

Here's what I mean by that. For example, if someone on your team has great analytical skills and those analytical skills help them make careful decisions, a bad way to manage them is to encourage them to decide from their gut instinct and move quicker.

You're probably laughing right now saying, 'Well, that's obvious!' But it wasn't obvious to me. I would watch the people that did those things and tell them, 'Hey, can't you just go a little faster? Can't you just feel this is the right way to do it?' They would look at me like I was a person from another planet. Frankly, I think I *was* from another planet in their eyes.

I learned that it won't work when you try to give them that type of suggestion.

Let me give you another example where I was terrible. I had an employee who hated making mistakes, and because they didn't want any mistakes they would check and re-check their work, especially if they knew I was going to review it. They would take too much time to get a project done because they would check and re-check to be sure it was perfect.

Well, let me tell you it doesn't work if you say, 'Hey, I know you like to get it right and make it perfect every time, but I'm in a hurry and I just want to see your rough draft.'

You can't do that, because they feel that asking them for their rough draft is opening them up to mistakes and criticism. It absolutely drives them bonkers. So don't do that. That's trying to make somebody into a human being that they weren't meant to be. It doesn't work, and it will never work.

As managers, we've got a job to do. We've got people that we must utilize to get things done because we can't do it all ourselves. The fact is, we often tell people that it's up to them to adjust and see the world our way. We get in a hurry and we think the short cut is to say, 'Look, let's not have the conversation any longer. I don't want to go there. I just want you to get finished. I want you to do this and do it my way.'

When we try to get people to adjust to the world our way what we are doing is filling them with negative energy. Let's discuss this, because it is not something that most managers have a concept of.

This starts when we are children. When we are young we are told, 'No, don't do that. No you can't do that. No you can't say that,' if you can remember. Maybe you have children of your own, and as a parent you don't want to do the wrong thing. So, we tell our children, 'No, don't do that. No, you can't do that. No, you can't say that.'

The fact is we repeat 'no, no, no' all the time. As a matter of fact, studies have shown that we hear the word 'no' eight times as much as we hear the word 'yes.'

What does that mean? It means that we are filling up these little minds with negative energy. As a good parent, it is necessary to some degree.

But we could impact our children and ourselves if we would focus on increasing the number of times we tell people 'yes.' Give them positive reinforcement because that 8:1 ratio is what they've grown up with. They are going to take that negative 8:1 ratio into the job. They are now your employee and your job is to get them to do the work.

They are carrying all that negative energy inside their brain – their subconscious – and they do it all their lives. Science proves that negative thoughts take up twice as much space in our brain as do positive thoughts. Think about that – twice as much space in our brain as positive thoughts.

It is because our brain is designed to protect us from danger, and we need to be protected. We need our brain and our subconscious to protect us from a hot fire and burning coals. But all the negative energy we're using gives our brain the ability to pull out negative memories faster when we are in an emergency. It allows us to run so that we can avoid the danger.

In one sense that is a good thing. But on the other hand, here you come as a manager and leader, and you're trying to manage people to do what you need them to do and to do it the way you want them to do it.

Let me ask you a question. What are we actually telling these employees? We're tell-ing their brain there is danger in not doing things the way that you and I tell them to do it. That builds up a protective wall inside their mind, and it affects their productivity.

Eventually we will have filled their brain with so much negative energy that the employee will shut down any semblance of creativity and decision making. They will decide slower, or they will defer everything to you as their manager.

If you have someone who is coming to you right now for everything, the worst thing you could do is tell them they shouldn't be coming to you all the time. That fills their mind with even more negative energy. You'll shut them down even more.

That's not the way to reach them. When you've reached the point where they are deferring everything, you can forget about goals. You'll be lucky if they are remotely close to achieving their goals.

I need to speak for just a moment to men only. The fact is, most men believe, and to a good degree we are taught, that we can fix anything. To put it bluntly, this is just plain dumb thinking.

Now ladies, I'm glad that most of you don't have this encumbrance. You know you can't fix everything (no one can), so you are not going to try like we males will.

Today I know that I can't fix everything. I have limited 'fixing' skills. For example, if you were to come to me and say, 'Hey, Steve – I'd like you to fix my car's engine,' I'd have no idea where to start much less how to fix it. I couldn't do it.

We know and understand this about most things, but we don't always carry that knowledge with us to work. We believe that because we are a manager and boss we can 'fix' people to do things the way we want them to.

The fact is, we may have received directives from our boss to fix somebody.

Let me give you an example from my own career. I had a boss who told me I had to fix a certain person. He told me that their attitude was affecting other people and if I couldn't fix them I should fire them.

But like all stories, there were two sides. The other side of the story was that this employee was productive and I couldn't afford to lose them. However, if this situation had occurred early in my career, let me tell you what I would have done.

I would have gone straight to them, and in no uncertain terms I would have given them their marching orders. I would have told them they were being disruptive; they were affecting everyone else and they had to stop right away. I would have filled their mind with so much negative energy and fear that nothing good would have resulted.

I would have dared them to disagree with me. Most likely I would have fired them anyway, just because I knew they would eventually break down and they would do exactly what I told them not to do.

But instead, I was later in my career, so I stopped and thought about it. I knew what I had been directed to do wasn't going to work. It wasn't the right approach for this person. I wanted this person to stay productive, and I knew I couldn't fix them.

So, what was the problem? The problem was that this employee had no idea of how other people perceived them. They had no concept of it.

Instead of approaching it from a negative standpoint, I approached it from a positive standpoint. We discussed how we could get people that were pushing back in the organization to be more cooperative. I used examples of behavior that would and wouldn't work. Before long the employee understood there was a different way they could go about doing things.

They had never thought about approaching people that way. They wanted to begin trying that idea because what they were doing wasn't working.

They knew it wasn't working, but they didn't know what to do about it. Once we discussed it from a standpoint of how we can get other people to work more easily with us, they wanted to put some energy into it. They wanted to change the perception that people had of them. They didn't want to be viewed as a negative person.

The whole dynamic had now changed. This time it was now both of us working on a problem and not me working on them as an individual. I wasn't trying to fix them.

It made a huge difference in the person's attitude and what a difference it made in the perception other people had of them. Suddenly it was like a new human being came to work.

I was asked, "What did you do to fix them?" I didn't do a thing. I can't fix anybody.

That is a great example to learn from, and we can take it deeper if you're committed to doing that. Science proves that all of us have certain behavioral strengths. Some of us are decisive. Some of us are proactive. Some of us are great at team building. Team builders are great at reducing tension and friction in a room.

Some people make decisions carefully and are very focused on producing a great result. Sometimes people make decisions quickly, and although their work may not be as exacting, they're able to take advantage of new opportunities because they move quickly.

It is up to us as leaders to understand what the strengths of each person are. Think about each person on your team and consider what their top 3 or 4 strengths are. Write them down.

For every team member, you ought to have your own personal notes. Every person on your team has at least 3 or 4 things they are good at. If they don't then you've probably put them in the wrong job. Likely this will be the reason for future turnover anyway.

It is likely you'll have someone who is disruptive to your team. Understand what their top 3 or 4 strengths are. Get to know them. Draw upon those strengths in every interaction you have with that person.

Let me encourage you – don't waste time focusing on the negative. When you focus on the negative it won't get the results that you want. Here's why.

Your job as leader is not to criticize. Your job is to lead, motivate and inspire. You will never lead, motivate or inspire anyone by making them feel stupid, worthless and ignorant. You won't lead anybody that way.

The next time you hear yourself saying or thinking the words, 'If you would just listen I could fix you and your problems,' I hope you will pause and take a deep breath. Take a moment and think about how to change that situation by using the power of leading, motivating and inspiring that individual.

I promise that this is the key and it is the secret that all great leaders follow. If you do this I promise the results on your team are going to be outstanding. You're going to set yourself up for that next promotion, and that is going to result in more income for you and your family.

The good news is that when you are actively practicing this, you begin to realize it's not about the money. It's about how you feel about yourself and the way your team feels about you. When you practice this, they're going to be your greatest advocates. They are going to sell everybody on your great strengths.

And that, my friends, is a win-win! You're focusing on *their* strengths and they are focusing on *your* strengths.

CHAPTER NINE

There is nothing training cannot do. Nothing is above its reach. It can turn bad morals to good. It can destroy bad principles and recreate good ones. It can lift men to performing excellence.

Mark Twain

www.ManagerMojo.com

TRAINING IS SUCH A WASTE OF TIME

I've heard managers say this for years. "Training is such a waste of time." The problem is that what they're doing is repeating exactly what was said to them.

Here's what I mean. When I talk about training being a waste of time, I'm talking about you training your people. Far too many managers say it's just too much trouble.

Here's why I say you're just repeating what was done to you.

You were a great individual contributor. You did stuff well. You did it on your own. In other words, what you were doing is training yourself.

So you got promoted and guess what? You got no training again, and you're training yourself once more.

When you choose not to train your people because 'you figured it out yourself – let them do the same thing!' you're only doing exactly what was done to you. It is rinse and repeat. What we didn't get, we don't give to someone else.

Consequently, our people struggle because we aren't doing any kind of training. I want to encourage you to break this cycle so that you and your team can achieve maximum results.

The first thing to recognize is that not everyone is like you. Not understanding that was a big mistake for me. I thought everybody was like me. I thought they were as driven as I was. I thought they were as motivated as I was, and they would train themselves just like I did.

That was a huge mistaken assumption, because what I soon realized was that most people don't train themselves and they aren't going to. Some may, but the clear majority will not.

You see, some people need lots of time and attention to master a particular part of the job that could be just a walk in the park for you. It doesn't mean they are ignorant, lazy or disinterested (although I do admit that if they didn't show signs of improvement over a period of time it could mean those things.)

It is up to you to discern the difference between somebody who is just being lazy, ignorant or disinterested, and someone who just needs additional training. The problem is that most managers today spend so little time with each individual on their team that they know very little about those people.

You must be able to know your employees' strengths and their weaknesses. Weaknesses are the easy part. You can find out where someone is weak because it is evident. When stuff doesn't get done, you realize they are weak in that area. You learn that over time.

But I'll tell you, what people are good at, their strengths, are much more difficult to assess. They are more discrete. Strengths hide in their personality, behavior and performance. It takes a manager who is on top of his or her game to understand what somebody's strengths are, instead of just their weaknesses.

The very real fact is that you, as the leader, must invest time in each individual member of your team to understand their strengths.

Think about it like you did with your spouse or significant other. When you got to know them you didn't know what they were great at. You knew that you liked them. You knew that they looked good, they sounded good. But it was over time, that investment of time with one another, that you began to understand each person's strengths and each one's weaknesses.

When you are willing to invest the time in your team it makes training so much easier. You can modify what you train and how you train to fit the strengths of each person. The results will mirror that investment of your time in them.

I realize it is very unlikely that you are going to do this. You're not going to train people unless you understand the real reason training doesn't happen.

The big reason that managers don't train, in my opinion, is because they have the wrong mindset. Let's talk about what I mean by the 'right mindset.'

Training wasn't done for you, because the very real fact is that most people don't like the concept of having to train others. They think it is below them as a manager. They are saying to themselves, 'Why should I train? We've got trainers that do that kind of stuff.' They don't want to do it and they may believe they're not very good at it. That would be a cop out.

The problem is that they have the wrong mindset because they don't understand what training is. I want to encourage you is to consider changing your mindset, and I want you to start thinking of training as *teaching*.

Having the mindset of *teaching* someone changes your attitude about 'training.' Let me give you an example.

If you have children or you've watched children, you are likely familiar with this scenario. Let's say you're teaching one of your children how to ride a bike. As you know, it takes time to teach somebody how to ride a bike. You've got to show them; you've got to hold them up and you've got to be patient with them through the process.

If you are a parent, are you going to be irritated and call your child a loser if they happen to fall the very first time they ride that bike without the training wheels? Of course not!

You are going to be patient. You will take that extra time. You will even show them. You might say, 'Hey, watch me! Watch what I'm doing.' Then when they fall again and again, what are you going to do? You're going to keep encouraging them. You're going to keep teaching until they get it.

Before you know it, they can ride that bike, and what do we do then? We celebrate! What a proud moment it is. It's fun because that teaching has paid off. Now your precious child can ride.

If you brought that same teaching mentality to the job and you applied it to your team members, great things would happen. It would electrify the results of your team.

In case you haven't made the connection yet, if you want that next promotion, that higher position, that next big raise, you're going to get those things for one reason only – by the superior results your team has demonstrated. You get there by demonstrating that you have great *teaching* qualities.

This is what separates great leaders from average leaders. Great leaders understand that a certain level of failure is good because that is part of the teaching process. They step in and teach and they get that superior performance level because they fill in the blank, so to speak, for the team member.

Having the mindset of teaching is going to benefit you in many other ways. It's going to benefit you both physically and emotionally as an individual. It lowers your blood pressure. Things don't seem out of control because your mindset is on teaching and doing it step by step.

Additionally, it's going to improve your communication skills. When you are teaching you are going to clearly see what works and what doesn't. That will give you many more ways to approach people than you currently have.

Additionally, it's going to improve your sense of optimism. Why? You're going to see incremental results, and incremental results are the key to success. It is incremental performance and improvement over time that makes for winners and winning teams.

When you understand this, you'll no longer be one of those managers who doesn't get it. That's what people say about most managers today. They don't get it and they don't understand. Well, how can they when they don't even know their people? Once you understand the value of teaching, I promise, you're going to be a leader that other people want to follow.

Change your mindset from one of dictating and telling to being one of *teaching* and I promise that the investment you're putting into teaching and training will lift your results.

It's going to give you the life and career you want and need for your personal success.

CHAPTER TEN

Magic
Happens
When Goals
Are Achieved

MY GOALS ARE MORE IMPORTANT THAN YOURS!

From a title like that, you're probably wondering what I'm going to talk about in regards to goals. Does that mean I'm against them?

No, goals are exceptionally important. They are important for all of us, both personally and in business. But goals by themselves can be a deterrent to people. If you don't believe what I'm talking about, just consider what happens when people set New Year's resolutions.

New Year's resolutions are supposed to be goals, but what they wind up being is a wish list – I wish I would lose more weight, or I wish I could get up earlier. It becomes a never-ending wish list that people don't really intend to keep. After 3-4 weeks, most people don't even remember they set a resolution. So, it's not truly a goal.

A goal is much, much more important than that. As human beings, we all need goals to strive for, so when I say 'my goals are more important than yours,' what I'm referring to is the way we often do things in leadership within our companies.

You see, we know that goals are important, but I must share with you that I believe both the setting of goals, meaning the way we actually set goals in our companies, and the way that we share those goals with our employees is one of the most mishandled tasks that managers do, and they do it all the time.

The reason we mishandle it is because we're unaware of what is going on when we start talking about goals. When we do share corporate goals, we do it wrong and people don't buy into it.

Let me talk more specifically. What am I really talking about?

When we set corporate goals, here is what usually happens. Senior management starts by figuring out what the objectives are for the company. They have a strategy and they want to execute on that strategy. They know what the metrics are that they need to manage to. They work very hard understanding those metrics, and they start handing down those corporate goals, or that set of metrics, to every manager.

In most companies, very little input has been received from the bottom up with input on those objectives. The reason is because the job of the CEO and the senior leadership team is to determine what's best for the overall corporation. Sometimes people don't understand what that strategy is because they don't know what the finances are or overall where the company is going. Maybe they are trying to change direction.

There may be some input, but not a tremendous amount has been given, and it is usually only at the higher levels. So, the further down in the organization you happen to be as a leader, the less input you've had in those goals.

Here's what happens. Once those goals are handed down, psychologically no one considers them a goal. They consider them their marching orders. In other words, it's what I'm going to be held accountable for to be considered successful in my job.

This same process is repeated at every level of leadership, all the way down to the line management team. There has been very little input at each level, and every level considers the goals their personal marching orders. It's what I've got to do at my level to be considered a success.

In addition to all of this, the line managers, the people closest to the employees doing the job, are expected to 'manage to those goals'. Often what 'manage to the goals' means is that you are expected as the front level manager and leader to harass or hold accountable your direct reports to meet those metrics.

On and on it goes. We hand down goals. If you start to look at this process and analyze it on an honest basis, you'll find out why I came up with this section's title "My Goals Are More Important than Yours!"

What top down, handed down, marching orders are saying is that the goals I'm giving you are more important than whatever you possibly could be thinking the goal should be. Here's how I'm going to measure you, here's what you've got to do, here are your marching orders and if you don't succeed in them then you're going to be held accountable.

It sets up a very poor psychological connection to the goals themselves. For those of you on the front line, I get it. I understand that your job is implementation, and I know that you don't often get a lot of input in those goals. You're held accountable as a manager and a leader to make sure you get the result.

Here's the teaching point that I want you to understand. You can change the mindset of your direct reports, no matter what level you are, if you understand a few key things.

The first thing I want you to recognize is that when you hand down goals with little or no input from the individual receiving those goals, there will be little or no buy in.

In other words, it's just numbers on a piece of paper. They aren't buying into it. They are saying 'OK that's what I've got to do.'

Understand that when you hand them down that psychologically you've made no connection with that individual. The employee will look at those goals and say OK. Or they may push back. I'm sure all of you have had the type of conversation where the employee doesn't buy in. You may get a little buy in, but not any real commitment. That is the first thing to understand.

The second thing to understand is that your employees can't and don't buy in because the goals don't link to their personal needs. In other words, the only way they connect personally is for the sole purpose of keeping the job that they have and keeping you as their manager off their back.

They can't buy into it because there is no personal connection. The goals came down impersonally, they were delivered impersonally and it didn't matter what that individual thought, needed or wanted. Psychologically not only did you not get any commitment or buy-in, they don't even get it. They don't see any connection to their personal life and that is often a huge discon-nect.

If that's not bad enough, the third thing you should understand is that top-down goals aren't goals. This is important, so make a note of it. What these metrics – 'goals' – have become is their *minimum level of performance*.

In other words, what has happened is rather than setting goals that people are commit-ted to, where they buy in, understand and connect the goals to themselves, it becomes a minimum level of performance. You as a leader are starting behind the eight ball regarding motivation, because there will be some employees who will look at those goals and say, 'Hey, no big deal. I can do that. I got it. No problem.' And what they will do is give you the minimum level of effort just to get those goals attained, to keep you off their back and to make sure they look good on the corporate ladder.

You may also have those employees who look at the goals as minimum levels of performance and maybe they'll say some-thing like (or behave like), "Well, I don't even care. This company doesn't care about me. They don't care about what I'm thinking." Then you've got an even bigger problem, because now you've got a disengaged team member.

Let me share a story that I've experienced to give you an idea of what I'm talking about. I had the privilege I guess you could say, of being part of a team that got goals handed down to them. We were a high-profile sales team of highly trained people. We had high profile clients, and we knew exactly what we were supposed to do.

We were at a level of responsibility where we had proven ourselves. We were top performers. We provided lots of revenue to the company, and we were in a position where we understood the business very well. We understood our customers, and we wanted to relate to the goals and objectives that came down from senior management.

But when we received these top-down goals it was almost laughable, because they were simply pie in the sky. Every single one of us knew that the goals didn't reflect what the marketplace was telling us.

Unfortunately, a couple of the guys took it personally. They got very upset. What happens when people get upset? They started having coffee sessions off site.

You know what that is. It's just a gripe session. They got everyone together and said, "What are we going to do about this? This is stupid. This is nuts. This is crazy. What are we going to do?"

Of course, it was counter-productive. Not only did they not buy into the goals; they were wasting everybody's time talking about something they couldn't change. They were going about it the wrong way.

You could there was a disconnection from the goals. It was the company saying, 'Look we don't care about your contribution and who you are. This is what you've got to do. Our own manager didn't communicate except to tell us, "This is what it is. I don't like it, but this is what it is. Everybody has to deal with it."

It set the wrong tone for the year, and I know you've probably had a similar experience. That's not effective goal setting, and it's not the way to connect with people. It's not how you're going to get their best. That's not how you're going to be the leader that others are going to want to follow.

That's not how you're going to be able to exercise your mojo.

The fundamental point here is that it is not up to the leadership above, and it's not up to those objectives, to get people charged up. The reason no one was charged up was because they couldn't make sense of what the company goals were in connection to their *personal* objectives.

In my example, many of the guys totally disconnected and we lost some good people. They took the attitude that the goals didn't relate to what they wanted to do in their life, and therefore they went off to do something else.

Whenever goals are presented in this fashion, it is so important for you as a leader with mojo to understand the motivations of every member of your team. It is much more valuable when you understand what's motivating each individual to perform at their best.

Yet I find most leaders and managers don't understand what's going on inside the minds of their people. They just want them to do their job and not give them a lot of problems or much feedback. They never truly *connect*.

Here's a key point, and please make a note of this. People want and need to connect psychologically to their work and personal life to do their best. You see, we spend most of our waking days at work. If you happen to be a leader in the United States, you understand what I'm talking about. Unlike other parts of the world, people that are in a leadership capacity in the United States are regularly working 55 - 60-hour work weeks. We are spending the majority of our waking hours at work.

We actually develop two lives, and our employees develop two lives. One of our lives is consuming most of our day because we are pursuing our job in order to get a paycheck. Our second life occurs when we finally leave the job and go home. That's when we get to do what we *really* love. We have this split personality if you will, and a split set of goals and objectives that don't motivate us when we are at work.

Sadly, many people live their entire lives doing just this. They go to work and they meet the minimum standard, because they know in their heart that their managers don't really care about their input. They don't really care what their personal goals are, and so they learn quickly not to share their personal goals. They don't share what they want to get done, and they do the minimum level to keep everyone off their back and keep the paycheck coming home.

Instead of doing things this way, let me give you a few things you can try and implement to get buy-in to company goals. There are three simple steps.

1) What I encourage you to do, if you want to be a leader others want to follow, is to understand the personal goals of every employee that works for you. Know what their dreams are. What are their ambitions? What level at work do they desire to reach? What are they willing to invest of themselves to achieve those desires?

In other words, you need to have meaning-ful conversations with each team member, and you need to be sincere about it. If you're not, they're not going to share with you. They'll say they don't have any goals, but what they're telling you is they don't trust you to understand what they want to do.

So many people are just there to get a paycheck. They don't like the job and they don't like the company, but they've got to have a job. They are hoping that eventually they can do what they love somewhere else.

What you get is the minimum level, because you don't understand what their personal goals are.

So, step #1 is to get to know each person really, really well. That requires a time commitment, but it is worth it!

2) The second thing you can do as a leader, once you understand their personal goals, is to connect the ambitions they have personally to the goals of the company. When you understand their goals, often you can connect them to company goals. The company goals then become a guide, a benchmark they will blow away because they are motivated by the right reasons.

Here is an example of what I'm trying to explain. An employee shares that they want to be two levels above where they are right now, and they want to be there in three years. They want to know what they've got to do to achieve that. You could clearly show them what they would have to achieve to be ranked in that top quartile, to be considered for the next promotion and the promotion after that.

Share with them how you did it, how you got ahead and how you plan to move forward. That will show leadership and real concern. You'll be able to tie the company goals into their personal ambitions.

3) Once you've begun to tie their ambitions to goals and you connect the dots, so to speak, you want to develop a plan with the employee of what they can and should do. You also want to include what you as the leader can and should do to help them achieve the objective.

When you show commitment to somebody and real concern for their personal goals, as well as corporate goals, suddenly the company goals don't become so impersonal. It puts them in a different light from being a minimum standard to being a standard that says 'I need to exceed this because my personal goal is to move to this level.' When you get that type of buy-in from your people, great things happen.

I'm not saying that every single person on your team is going to buy in, that they want a promotion and want to succeed. In fact, statistics show that two out of ten people do most of the work anyway. They provide 80% of the results. The fact is, if you motivated two, three or five people on your team to do outstanding results, guess what you are going to look like as a leader. You're going to be an outstanding leader!

Your goal is to change that 80/20 rule in your favor. You want 80% of your team achieving astronomical results. When that happens, you're a killer leader and you're the kind of guy or gal that is going to get promoted, recognized and rewarded. That's when you're really exercising your mojo and your leadership capability.

I hope that has been helpful. If you follow those three steps you will be light years ahead of most managers and leaders. It would be your team that's leading the pack and not your peer's.

Most people won't use this approach. They don't want to have this type of personal connection and discussion. But I believe if you do, you're going to get the rewards of it.

Company goals are your goals as a manager. They can never superimpose their will over an employee. People work by choice, so for you to get the best from your team you need to truly understand their motivation. You can't fake that. You must *know* it. In order for you to know it you should *invest* in them if you want the best results.

Change the philosophy to become one that says, 'All our goals are important. We are all great contributors in this thing we call work.'

SUMMARY

Begin focusing on these 10 steps today. Use this book as your game plan to start having great, powerful one-on-ones, teach, and connect, and I promise you're going to make a tremendous impact on the results of you and your team.

If you want to learn more about being a Manager with Mojo, subscribe to my twice-weekly podcast, *Manager Mojo with Steve Caldwell*. You can do that at:

https://managermojo.com/category/podcast/.

Let's help people be the best they can be! I hope that you'll join with me, and ***let's rock the world!***

Your Next Step

Now that you have read the book, the next step is to take control of your leadership development. Go deeper at:

Mojo University
http://mojouniversity.com/

MORE ABOUT STEVE CALDWELL

 Steve Caldwell built a successful career and life on the backs of those who supported and helped him along the way – his real estate mentor, the boss who called for a meeting yet had the decision already made (yes, even good things come from poor situations), and countless others who stepped up to offer him a hand.

Now he's taking that support and passing it along to you. Take these seven key insights – plus three bonuses – and apply them to *your* life and career. They can be applied as successfully in your personal life as they can in business.

Be sure to connect with Steve on LinkedIn, Twitter and Facebook. You can find him at the addresses below. Remember to mention this book and let him know how it helped you. We also encourage you to leave a review on Amazon.

LinkedIn
http://mojou.me/LinkedInSteveCaldwell

Twitter
http://mojou.me/TwitterSteveCaldwell

Facebook
http://mojou.me/FacebookMgrMojo

When you visit the Manager Mojo Business Page on Facebook you will get all the latest Mojo by 'Liking' our page and participating in the conversation.

Now get busy and *Rock the World!*